Good Night Sky

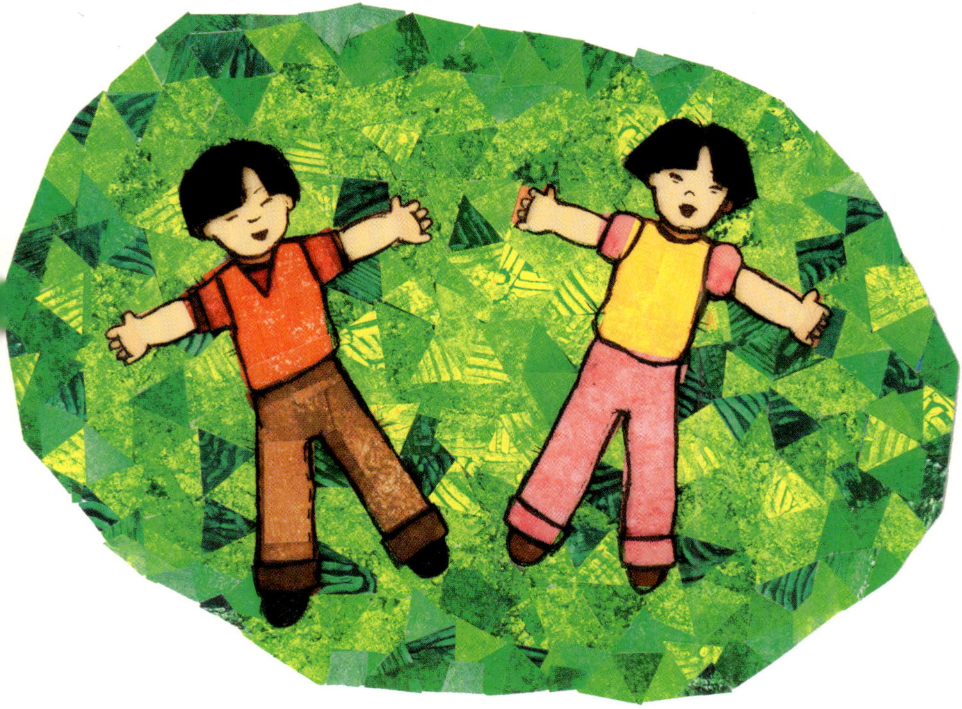

Story by Audrey Danforth and Jane Kennedy

Illustrations by Christy S. Terry

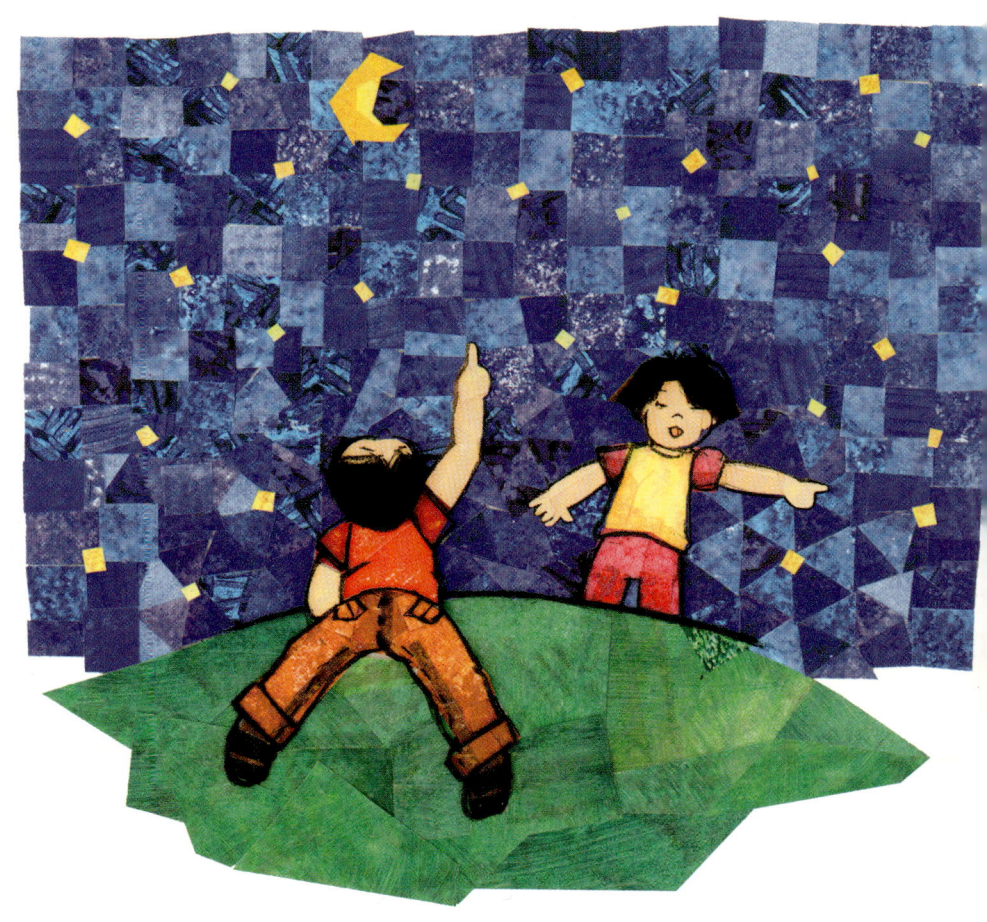

See the moon.

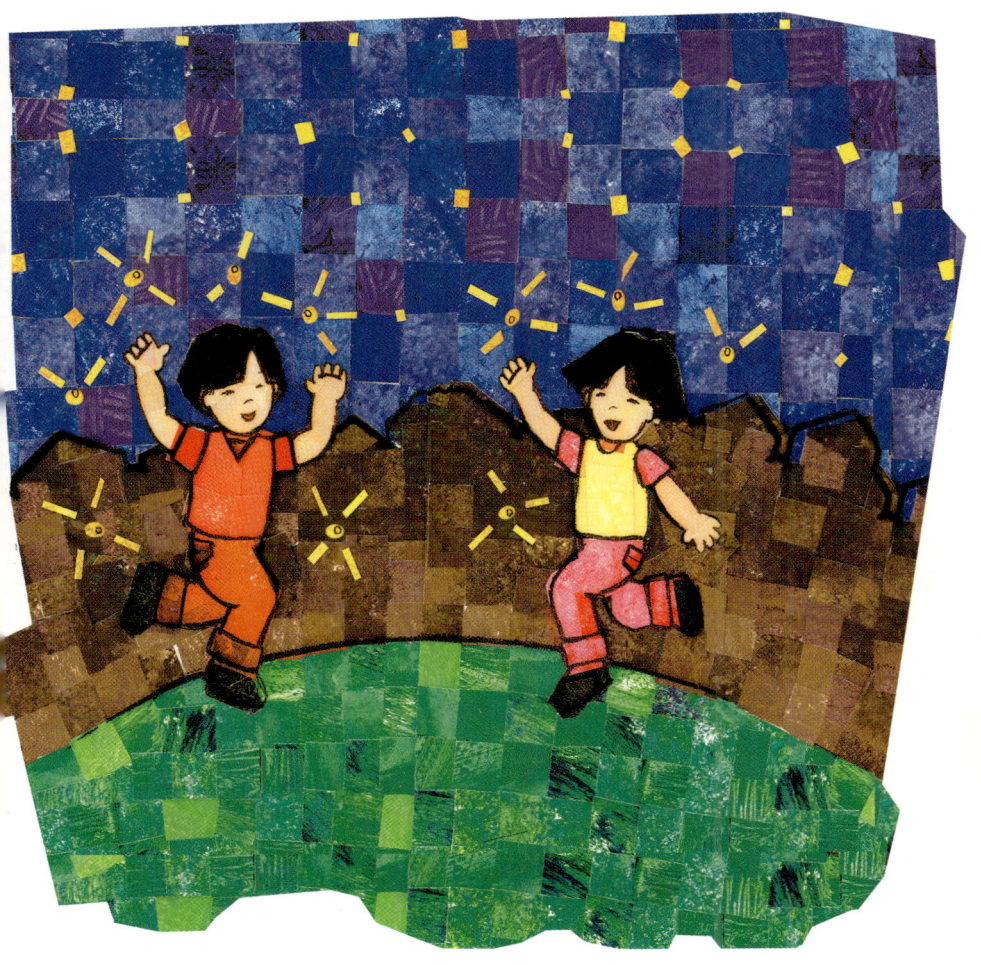

I can see the fireflies too.

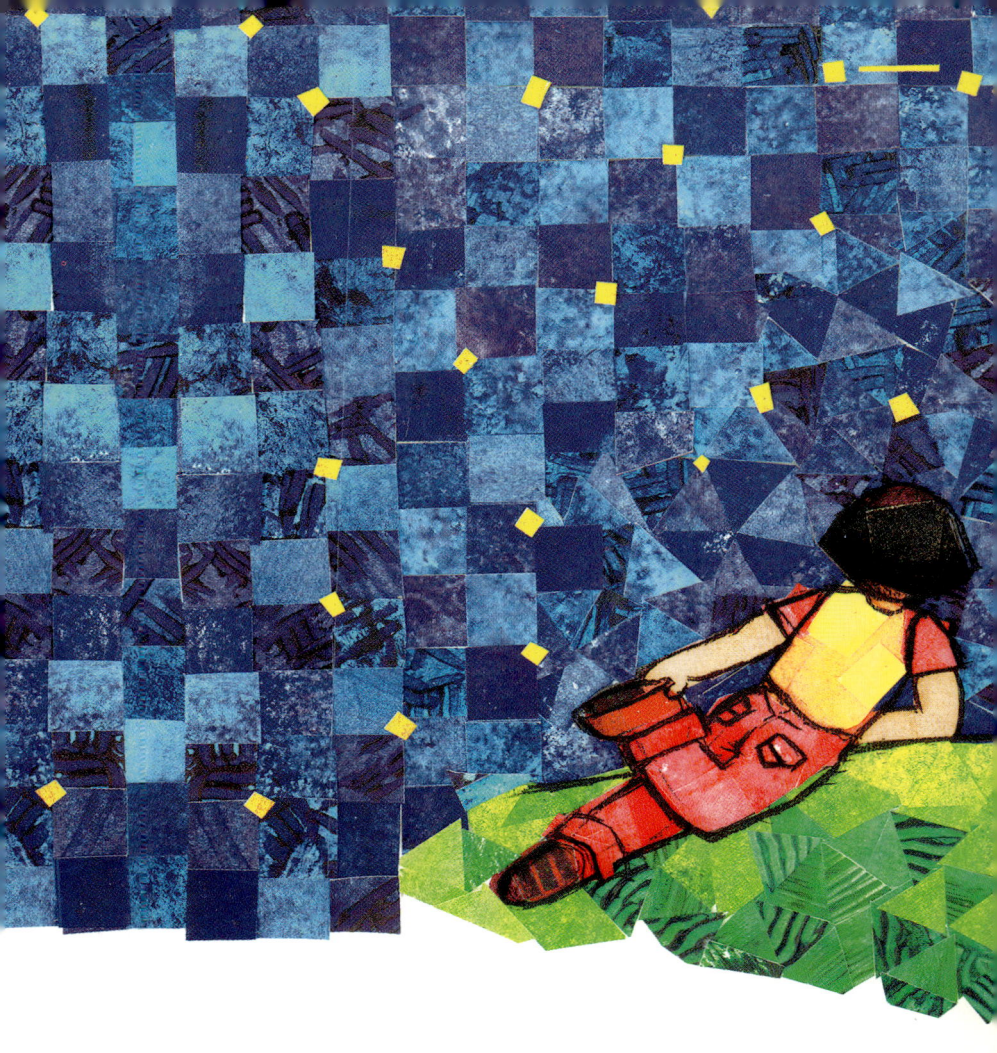

I can see the stars.

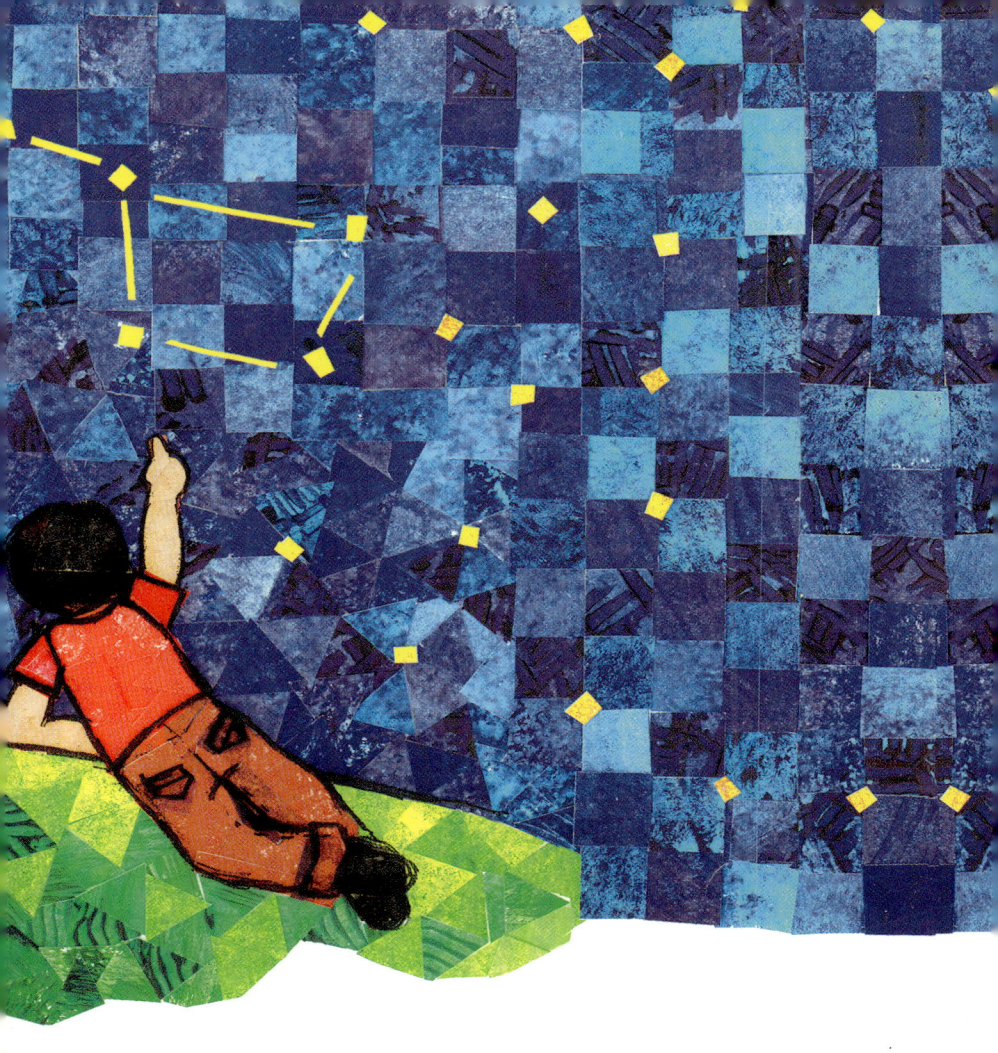

Can you see the Big Dipper?

5

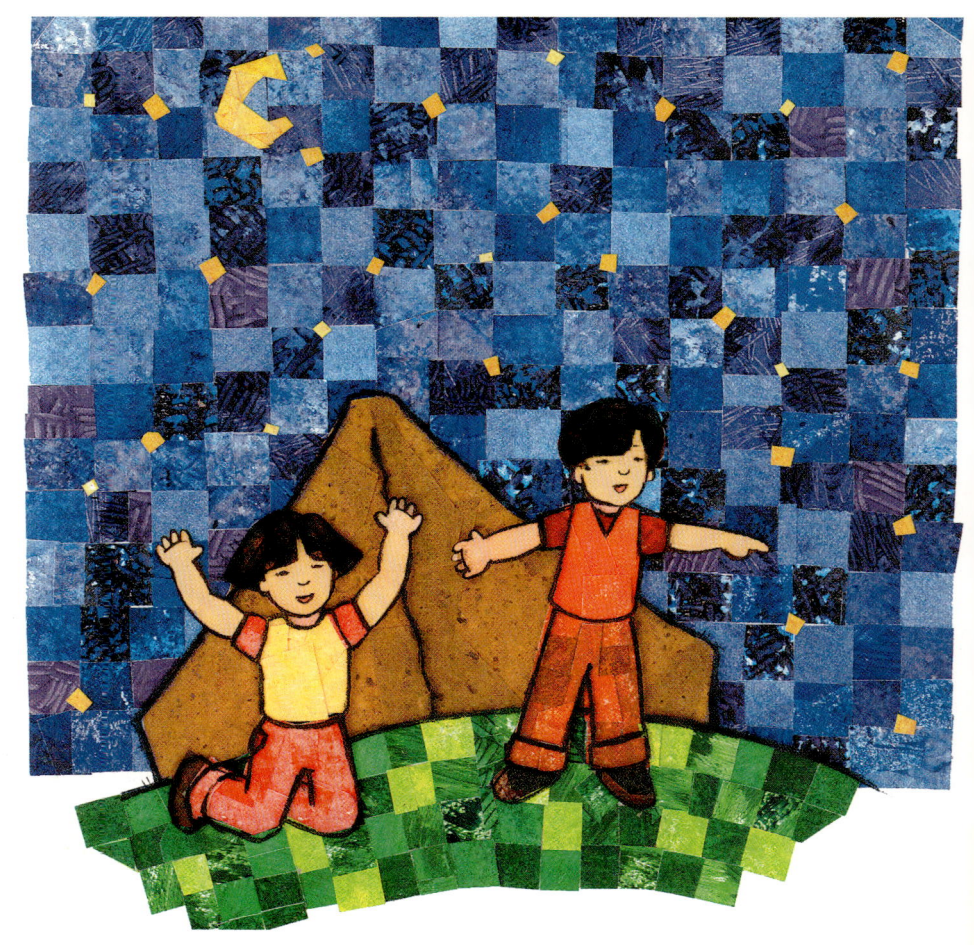

I can see a light.

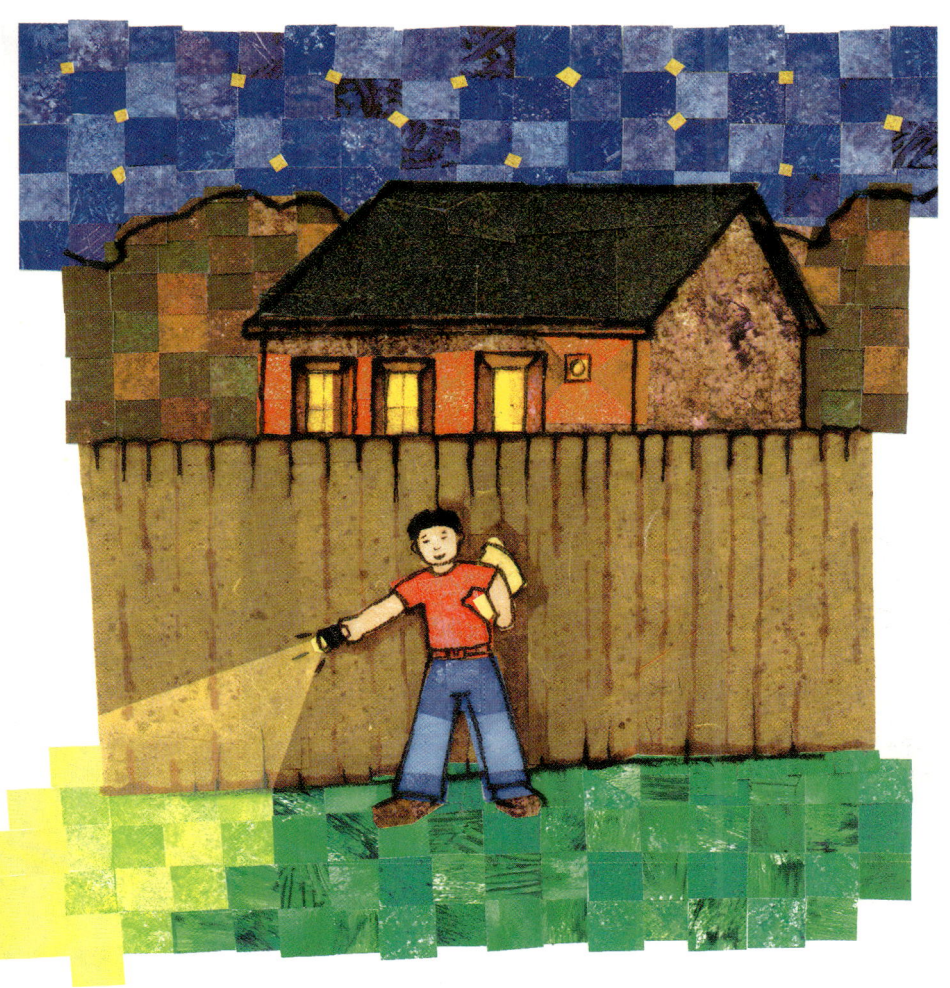

I can see Dad!

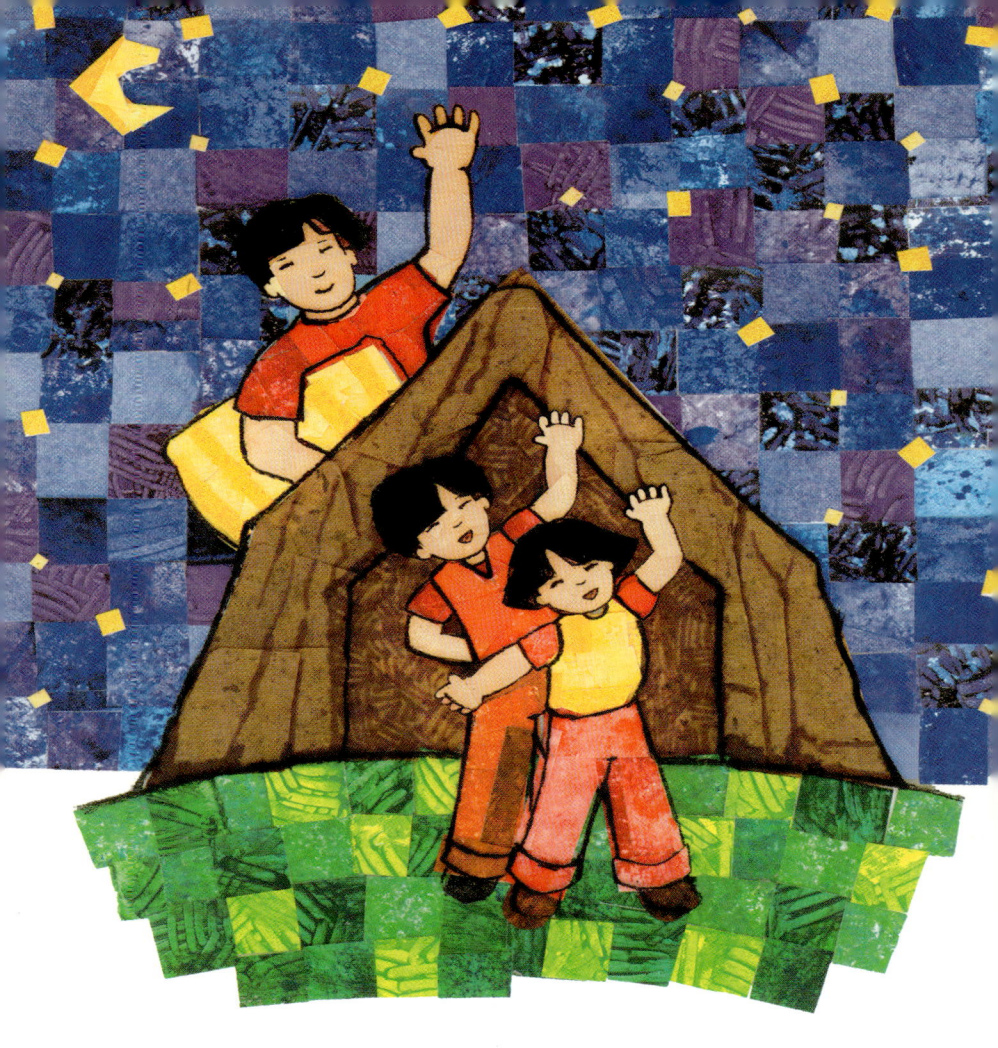

Good night sky.